# The Orgreav

## Poems b<sub></sub> William Hershaw

## Images by Les McConnell

*Well now, you rich! Lament, weep for the miseries that are coming to you... It was you who condemned the upright and killed them; they offered you no resistance.*

—James 5:1 and 6

*Orgreave led to a massive breakdown of trust in the police in the former mining communities (and indeed more widely) and this continues today among the children, grandchildren, families and friends of the miners. Orgreave marked a turning point in the policing of public protest. It sent a message to the police that they could employ violence and lies with impunity.*

*With the Conservative Government's current raft of policing and other legislation aiming to further restrict our rights and freedoms, the right to protest in public is in serious danger.*

—Orgreave Truth and Justice Campaign

First published 2024 by **Culture Matters**.
**Culture Matters** promotes cultural democracy.
See www.culturematters.org.uk


Text copyright © William Hershaw
Cover image and all other images © Les McConnell
Edited by Mike Quille
Layout and typesetting by Alan Morrison

ISBN: 978-1-912710-67-6

# Contents

# Introduction

## By William Hershaw

The Battle of Orgreave took place on 18th of June 1984, during the Miners' Strike at a British steel coking plant at Orgreave, near Rotherham in South Yorkshire. Picketing miners from the Nation Union of Mineworkers were confronted and attacked by South Yorkshire Police and members of other police forces, including the Metropolitan Police Force.

At the time, the ensuing violence was largely blamed by the media and the Tory Government on the actions of the miners. In the years since, more and more evidence has come to light indicating that the confrontation and subsequent mass arrests were part of the government plan to close pits, destroy the NUM and thus defeat the wider trade union movement. The miners' cause —of fighting to save jobs and the mining communities—has been shown to be true, and the Tory account that they were "defending freedom" shown to be a pack of lies. Unsurprisingly, a full official inquiry into what happened at Orgreave has been continually denied in the ensuing years.

Orgreave was thus much more than a physical confrontation. It was a battle of ideas, a class struggle, and a political and moral battle about the future. Unfortunately, the wrong side won, that day.

Orgreave was pivotal in shaping subsequent UK politics, social history and culture. The Thatcher government's victory over the miners signalled the start of a shift toward neoliberal, right-wing ideas and policies that have continued to set agendas and create misery to this day for working people. It was a victory for a divisive culture of greed and selfishness, of the worship of profit and the denigration of communal values of fairness, equality, support and care for individuals and communities. It was Thatcher who proclaimed glibly that there was no such thing as society, and that the individual only had a duty to look after herself/himself.

The bitter memories that Orgreave evokes are still alive for many. Its legacy, the physical and mental scars of the industrial wasteland left by Tory policies, are still evident. While unfettered capitalism has now reached a point where the planet itself is at terrible risk and the argument for fossil fuels has become untenable, the politics of Orgreave are still highly relevant. Forty years after the Miners' Strike the leader of the UK Labour party felt the need to publicly praise Thatcher's leadership. This was an insult to the communities who suffered under her, and conclusive proof of the UK's continuing lurch to the right.

i

So how will Orgreave be remembered, and how will its lessons be passed on to younger generations? In as many ways as possible, I hope. *The Orgreave Stations* is a poem sequence, not a documentary account. Its structure is based on the traditional form of the Stations of the Cross—the biblical accounts of Christ's journey from Gethsemane to his crucifixion at Golgotha, including his arrest, judgement, torture and execution as 'the enemy within'—a political enemy of the Roman state. In writing my account of Orgreave in this way, I hope that the symbolic religious imagery will help readers to appreciate not only the literal facts of what happened during the Miners' Strike, but the full moral implications of what the actions meant.

Because at the heart of the Battle of Orgreave lies the question of moral choices. There were choices to be made, about using the might of the state (the police and judiciary) and the media to maintain a position of wealth and power for the ruling class, or being prepared to make personal sacrifices and take the consequences, for the sake of the community and the working class. The fact that the former won the battle and the latter was not supported by many, made me ask questions then and ever since: how can you be a Christian and a Tory? Can you be a Christian and not a socialist? Who are Christians but mealy-mouthed liberals who sit on the fence while the meek and the weak get bullied and mugged? The wrong moral choices, made at Orgreave, during the Strike, and afterwards, have resulted in the political culture and system we see today—an amoral one totally lacking in empathy and support for working people and their communities.

At this point, let me make a declaration of personal interest. In Fife, where I lived and where members of my family were miners, we had memories and a long history of previous strikes and class-based politics. Back in 1921 and 1926 the government in London brought the Army into Central Fife, to quell the striking miners. The notorious Black and Tans were sent into Cowdenbeath and Lochgelly, to attack mining communities, arrest and beat up the populace, especially trade union officials and leaders. Machine-gun posts were set up, aimed at women and children in the street; houses were broken into in the middle of the night and strikers dragged off to be sentenced. Many of these same miners had fought in World War One—yet Churchill sanctioned all this. The period is depicted brilliantly in Robert Rae's groundbreaking film *The Happy Lands*, itself based on Cardenden miner poet/playwright Joe Corrie's *In Time of Strife*, performed by the Bowhill Players.

Many Scottish miners travelled to Orgreave on hearing Scargill's call for solidarity. My grandad, a miner at High Valleyfield Pit, told me that NUM members were well used to harassment from the police by then. Phones were tapped, and sometimes a striking miner would be stopped a few yards from his house, when he left it to join a picket line.

Not in the case of Orgreave, though. The Fifers were stopped at roadblocks, questioned as to their purpose, then genially waved on. On one occasion they were even given helpful advice on shortcuts to avoid further stoppages. The reason? It was a pre-planned ambush. They wanted as many miners as possible kettled in one place so they could show them who was in charge. Following that it was arrest, being punched and kicked, falsified charges, maximum sentences, and having a criminal record for the rest of your life.

And so it got worse. If this corrupt and rotten system had put half as much effort and resources into tackling issues like poverty, health and education, we would be living in a better, fairer world by now. Instead, the Tories were fixated on bringing down the Left and in the process turned whole swathes of the country into hopelessly impoverished reservations. They were prepared to spend a fortune to attack fellow citizens, when it would have been cheaper to give them jobs and keep the pits open. They did this in plain sight—and not enough people called them out.

*The Orgreave Stations* is a successor to my previous book *The Sair Road*, published by Grace Note Publications, concerning the struggles of the mining communities in my native Fife. Both are illustrated brilliantly by my longtime collaborator, the artist Les McConnell. My thanks go also to Jim Aitken for his perceptive criticism and positive advice. The present book would not have reached print without the huge shift put in by Culture Matters editor Mike Quille, who provided not only his experience, guidance, encouragement and editing skills, but helped steer the project, keeping me firmly focused on the job at hand.

Orgreave wasn't just a battle—it was part of an ongoing war, an assault on our liberty and values. It goes on, so the story of Orgreave must be remembered and retold, over and over. Truth and justice will prevail.

# Early Doors: At the Cross

*By the sweat of your face you shall eat bread, till you return to the ground, for out of it you were taken; for you are dust, and to dust you shall return.*

—Genesis 3:19

When the Co-op clock strikes midnight,
there's a stirring of the hosts:
the hearse-black bus of the back-shift men,
or the pit-boots of homeward ghosts?

Is it the pithead lassies,
who sorted the lumps from the dross?
Or the jingling of thirty pennies
gambled at pitch and toss?

The wind girns through the empty streets,
lamenting aye the cost:
the town's unquiet, remembering
the Happyland it lost.

At dawn there's a greying in the east:
though the resonances thrum,
though the grievanced ghosts still work their shifts,
a new Happyland will come.

## Station 1: The Road to Gethsemane Allotments

*You shall love your neighbour as yourself.*

—Mark, 12:31

"Heads up, comrades, all gathered here today,
Though it sticks in your throats, you'll hear me out!
Try to forgive them—love the lousy lot.
Bless them as they abuse and harm—deal them back good.
Pray for the pains in the arse—and those worse,
The greedy, liars, lawyers, bankers, frauds..."
Jesus spoke on the War Memorial steps,
Giving it large to the listening folk.
"My Dad was old school, fought too many wars,
Set in his ways, deaf to his wife and kids.
But time moves on—his day is in the past.
So here's a thought that you can all take home—
A concept bigger than any of us:
The greatest sacrifice is that of self!
I know you think I'm daft, just wittering on—
To love is hard without condition, love
Yourself, each other, enemies as well,
The sneak, the scab, Thatcher even, (jeers and catcalls),
The police, magistrates... you cannot choose.
It's all or nowt, this garden's meant for all—
So grow the marvellous gift, the flower of grace!
Think on your slag heap of faults, piled up high,
Before you hurl your neighbour down to Hell.
Our world is weeded with false controlling creeds,
Sly stories hatched by hateful hidden men
Just to get their way, so they can hold sway,
Raise ghouls of ghastly fears to paralyse,
Hold us beneath the thumb—aye, jam will come!
That's always been the line when there's no bread.
Might we not have contented lives, live well,
And live them now, enjoying our kind Earth—

Though none of us here own one ounce of it?
And yet we get no better than the beasts,
Chained to the shift and clock all day, brain-dead,
Too tired in the night to speak our thoughts,
Disenfranchised from life's precious joys.
Think on the stuff the heart and soul love most—
Peace, plenty, the price of a pint—happy days!
Let us work together and build it now.
And last, I ask just one more thing from you:
Bring the kids up right—our innocent lambs.
We brought them into this. Our days, our hope!
Make sure their lives are pit-propped with our love."

An unmarked car had parked to mark his card.
Its plain clothes driver hadn't heard the like.
"My guv'nor Herod will hear of this tripe."

## Station 2: Arrested

*"Father, if you are willing, take this cup from me; yet not my will, but yours be done." An angel from heaven appeared to him and strengthened him. And being in anguish, he prayed more earnestly, and his sweat was like drops of blood falling to the ground.*

—Luke 22:43

When Winter's miserable cold crept in,
When Jesus, depressed and full of doubts
Took himself down that bleak lonely road,
To Wigan Pier, Gethsemane allotments,
His spirit gone, his mind and body done,
He'd things to settle in his troubled mind.
But a deep dread, an eerie premonition,
A feeling in his blood of coming doom,
A darkness welling up inside his heart,
Caused beads of sweat to drop down from his brow.
"This is a brew that's sour to taste. I'll pass.
I'd rather leave this ale pot full for now.
Yet if this round's for me I'd better drink..."
Whispering voices would not let him rest.
He thought of his old Dad, still sorely missed,
And then his mates: Big Pete and Little Jack,
Kind Andy, Tom, Mattie, Si, Judas too—
All in their kip or supping down the club.
A special shout out for his dearest Mum,
Old Mary who had brought him to this world—
He loved them all. But was small love enough?
He doubted that he had the bottle needed,
Courage to ride the punches sure to come.
A fluttering of softness, a feather fell,
In silver moon light, pigeon or angel?
The sheds, raised beds and plots transformed with grace,
Then suddenly his heart was filled with peace.

The night was cold, the frozen seeds asleep,
Beneath the soil, to germinate in Spring.
A promise of a better time, a harvest:
For here was where he sowed and hoed and dug,
His troubled soul found solace in each shift,
And even in this coldest dark it did its work.
All miners feel the pull of what's denied:
Wide open space: the land, the air, the sky.
Licence to wander, to breath and go free,
Not crushed by the black stones of poverty,
To follow the lark instead of the gaffer's curse,
Forced to be locked in darkness underground
Like Ariel imprisoned in a tree.
And then he knew the journey he must take:
Down to hell inside the cage at break of day
To harrow that foul kingdom of naysay.

A heavy hand, a grasping shoulder grab:
"You're lifted, Trotsky—in the fucking van.
Your comrade, brother Judas turned a scab."

## Station 3: Condemned

*At daybreak the council of the elders of the people, both the chief priests and the teachers of the law, met together, and Jesus was led before them. "If you are the Messiah," they said, "Tell us."*

—Luke 22:66-67

The next day he was taken to their court,
Already judged by their *Sunhedrin, Mail,*
So-called free media and the BBC,
Sentence decided long before the trial
As ordered by Thatcher and MacGregor,
Hypocrites, scared he would defeat their plan.
All their attack dogs were unleashed on him.
All that he stood for galled, stuck in their craw:
*A Christian has to be a socialist.*
Though he stood quiet, he answered every charge.
They said his aim was chaos, harm,
They were defending democratic rights:
The old imperialist lie: divide and rule.
They claimed he'd tried to make himself a king—
There never was one less in thrall to crowns.
"Look at King Jesus of Orgreave!" they mocked.
Not bothered by their perjuries and lies
They sentenced him then threw him in their jail.

## Station 4: Big Pete

*After a little while, those standing there went up to Peter and said, "Surely you are one of them; your accent gives you away." Then he began to call down curses, and he swore to them, "I don't know the man!" Immediately a rooster crowed. Then Peter remembered the word Jesus had spoken.*

—Matthew 26:71-75

Before the sun rose and dayshift began
Big Pete went looking for his troubled pal.
He'd sworn to him whatever woes betide,
Through thick and thin, he'd always have his back.
Pete, full of life, though bald beneath his cap,
Aye loyal, straight, a grafter and good mate,
A guy to have beside you in a hole,
Ambushed by right-wing thugs or cutting coal,
Yet even he denied him: "I worry, look—
I cannot see a way to win this fight...
The papers say that Thatcher will not turn—
We should have put it to a vote to strike,
We're out to bring the country to its knees,
And though it's all a crock of made-up shite
There's even some in Labour who agree.
Some comrades have gone home, they need the dosh,
There's others never joined us from the off.
I read a bishop said the strike is wrong..."
Three times the cock crew in the still of dawn.

## Station 5: Judged by Pilate

*"Do you refuse to speak to me?" Pilate said. "Don't you realize I have power either to free you or to crucify you?" Jesus answered, "You would have no power over me if it were not given to you from above. Therefore the one who handed me over to you is guilty of a greater sin."*

—John 19:6-11

They stood upon a waste of broken lives,
A blasted nowhere slag heap without hope,
A line of coughing skulls on a frayed belt,
Grey nettles growing out the pithead rust.
Dark-suited, he took Jesus by the arm:
"You may be shocked, this landscape hurts me too,
But thankfully I see a better day,
These relics of the past all swept away.
The children of the future—they'll thank us
For getting rid of coal, they'll never fuss.
So let the miners die, they're halfway there,
A generation on, no one will care.
Be sensible - extinction paves the way.
I've come to make an offer, in good faith,
You see, I've kept a judging eye on you
And been impressed. Join us and have your say.
Instead of helping losers, help yourself.
A change is in the air, can you not tell?
Orgreave will be the point, long overdue,
To reassert our right, our might, the coup.
Too long the liberals have held their sway:
The right to strike, free grants, free meals, free speech,
Free this and that, an Open University!
The hope to have it all in easy reach,
Meanwhile the unions get to call the shots.
They've stretched the rope too far—and now it stops.
We'll reel you in, this time without release,
And if there's qualms or questions raised,

Who better than South Yorkshire Police
At changing evidence? Fine loyal cops,
We've got it organised right from the top.
Judges, media, everything well planned.
You'll get selected coverage on Sky—
This revolution will be privatised.
But know this son, we don't bear grudges long,
So come on board, there's room for those like you:
Talented, committed, who know the form.
You can be a stakeholder in days to come,
With dividends and add-ons—I'll run you through:
While raising up a cult of greed and self,
The rights of individuals will be shelved,
The richer that you are the less we'll tax,
Our vision is a floating offshore bank,
A new order's here, a future to forge,
Do it for Maggie, do it for Saint George!
But feel no pity for the underfed:
It's not like Orwell and Huxley said.
While lesser races make the things we need,
We'll dismantle the Health Service at some speed
They'll buy their council houses, get on bikes,
Their high streets full of bookies, phone shops, vapes
Tattoo parlours numbering the slaves,
Hierarchy and glass ceilings—that they love,
The chance to bow and scrape to those above.
And if they start to see through all our flannel
We'll blame it on the wogs crossing the Channel ...
We'll do the thinking and deciding from now on
And in the end, that's what they really want.
The Labour Party's gone—thanks and goodnight,
From now we're heading swiftly to the Right.
So make your mind up—now you've heard the plan.
I'll be back soon—I must go wash my hands.

And Comrade Jesus wept.

## Station 6: Jesus is Scourged and Crowned with Thorns

*Then Pilate took Jesus and had him flogged. The soldiers twisted together a crown of thorns and put it on his head. They clothed him in a purple robe and went up to him again and again, saying, "Hail, king of the Jews!" And they slapped him in the face.*

—John 19:1-3

And when the shameful bus approached the gates
A howl of anger rose up from the crowd.
The picket line rushed forward at the scabs,
To make their pent-up feelings heard and felt.
Then the police weighed in with horses, shields,
Brought batons down upon unfended heads,
Set dogs on them, put in the boot with glee.
Jesus of Orgreave was among the folk.
In cuffs, two coppers threw him in the van,
Locked him away behind their strong black doors.
That's where the boys in blue soon went to work:
They punched him, mocked him, swore and jeered and spat,
Centurions waved tenners in his face.
They shouted "commie scum" and boasted that,
"This kicking's just the start, there's more to come."

## Station 7: Jesus Takes Up His Cross

*Then Jesus said to his disciples, "If anyone desires to come after me, let him deny himself, and take up his cross, and follow me. For whoever desires to save his life will lose it, but whoever loses his life for my sake will find it."*

—Matthew 16:24-25

Jesus the union health and safety rep
Knocked on the pit manager's office door:
"We have concerns I have to raise with you:
Down there the ventilation's poor, no air,
We're breathing in lungfuls of choking dust,
It's far too hot, the explosion risk is high,"
The boss looked bored but listened with a sigh.
"It's safe enough—I've had the whole thing checked,
I put in a gob curtain at the headgate,
The flow-through air is fine so long's you lads
Don't skive, forget what you are there to do,
Make profit for us all, the company, you—
So don't blame me if anything goes bad.
A word of sound advice. I've seen your sort.
Out to create bother, always complain,
The union man who talks but digs no coal—
A better job than being on the dole.
Go back and say you've spoken, tell the men."
And Jesus had a choice to make, right there and then.

## Station 8: Simon of Cyrene

*"Carry each other's burdens, and in this way you will fulfill the law of Christ."*

—Galatians 6:2

Many years before that, in another pit,
The way was wet and steep and Jesus slipped.
Then Simon of Cyrene said, "That pit prop,
Give us an end—I'll help you shift this gear,
Far easier with four hands than with the two..."
They lifted it. What Simon said was right.
When they both worked as one, their load was light.

## Station 9: The Women

*A large number of people followed him, including women who mourned and wailed for him. Jesus turned and said to them, "Daughters of Jerusalem, do not weep for me; weep for yourselves and for your children."*

—Luke 23:27-28

Daughters of the kitchen, bang your pot lids,
For you and your husbands, for hungry kids,
Wake the conscience of the Government,
Hellbent to see you all put on the streets,
Intent to break your spirit, close your noise,
Furious at your will to make ends meet,
Your selflessness that shames their shallow lives,
Daughters and sisters, mothers and wives,
At home, fundraising, on the picket line,
With faith and love, strong women all of them,
With bacon butties building better men.
Women who were the first slaves, stand up proud,
Go wake the deaf and scream your suffering loud.

## Station 10: Crucifixion

*When they came to the place called the Skull, they crucified him there, along with the criminals—one on his right, the other on his left. Jesus said, "Father, forgive them, for they do not know what they are doing."*

—Luke 23:33-34

And Jesus crawled along wet wooden planks
That stretched over the abyss on two wires.
The infall gaped so vast, a hellish drop:
The Moss had sunk, the mine was choked with mud.
A miracle, no way to save those souls,
"We'll bring them to the surface or we'll die."
To find them quick, gasping in airless holes,
To dig them out the shit then bring them home
To light and life and air—a slim hope, yet
Without a hope what are you going to get?
But was it worth the agony, he thought?

## Station 11: The Good Thief

*Then he said, "Jesus, remember me when you come into your kingdom." Jesus answered him, "Truly I tell you, today you will be with me in paradise."*

—Luke 23:42-43

The idiot who took down contraband
Took roof and gear and mates down too.
All for a smoke. Survivors in the dark,
Among the twisted beams. Then Jesus spoke
To the young lad who stole his snap tin.
"We're trapped, we're fucked, but don't you worry son,
The theft of cheese and pickles is forgiven,
Have this water here—aye, my snap tin's yours.
Help is on its way, we'll win free soon, perk up.
Come Friday night you'll strut your stuff with Jean,
Steak pie and bingo down at the Miners' club."
The boy was fading and his spirit gone,
His hopes of any future had been killed.
"It may not come to you as much relief,
But down here in the dark we're all Good Thieves...
Well done, a smile! You've done us proud, hang on..."

27

## Station 12: Jesus Speaks with his Mother and a Disciple

*When Jesus saw his mother there, and the disciple whom he loved standing nearby, he said to her, "Woman, here is your son," and to the disciple, "Here is your mother." From that time on, this disciple took her into his home.*

—John 19:26-27

We never saw it, mother, had no clue,
It would always be thus, we had no doubts.
*Jesus was born in a post war dream,*
*Jesus was born in a council scheme.*
Jesus was born with the highest of hopes,
And those not like Jesus would get help to cope.
We drank free milk at school and never wondered.
With regional accents no longer rejected,
We made a mistake, thought we were accepted.
Somehow the poorhouse would become much kinder,
Unknowing they'd outsource it to Rwanda,
Unknowing how they'd geld our will to fight,
Unknowing they'd outlaw our right to strike.
When you and Joe got spliced after the war,
What had your sacrifice been all about?
Surely you had a part, a start, though poor,
Surely a stake in all that you'd fought for?

And then, years on, a thing no one foresaw,
A state that attacked its own helpless folk.
Dogs of war unleashed on communities,
To serve a selfish ideology,
And not just miners: women, bairns and old,
And all who stood against their evil will,
Their thirst to silence, subjugate and break.
And they alone knew all that was at stake
Well briefed on what the consequence would be:

Cultural and material poverty
For evermore, with never a Plan B.
A world to come of borrowing and debt,
Of hopelessness and poverty and hate.
Even black lung was better than that fate.
A government determined to reject
Society existed. No sense of nowt but gain,
Hell bent to hurt, when protect was their duty.
They broke the law with impunity:
*Orgreave was our bloody Calvary.*

I'm crucified, they've hung me out to dry,
If I survive all that they throw at me,
I'll be gone a while—moonlighting for God,
To go where I am needed is my job.
Meanwhile the team will take good care of you.
*Orgreave was our bloody Calvary.*

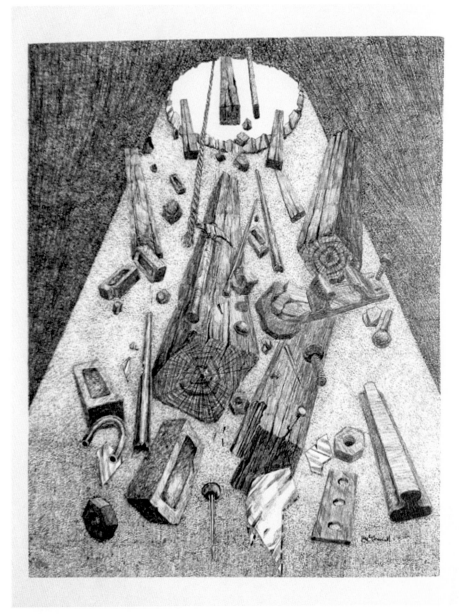

## Station 13: Death

*It was now about noon, and darkness came over the whole land until three in the afternoon, for the sun stopped shining. And the curtain of the temple was torn in two. Jesus called out with a loud voice, "Father, into your hands I commit my spirit." When he had said this, he breathed his last.*

—Luke 23:44-46

Profit's never mentioned at an inquest,
Ignored like pleas to deal with gas or flood.
Their pit props were cheap wood that snapped like bones,
You'd have a job to hang a scab from them.
That time the roof came down on Jesus' back
was only one of thousands down the years.
At Kellingley Joe Green was doing his bit,
Trying to turn back trucks when he was hit
Or Davie Jones outside the Ollerton mine:
A lorry bumped the kerb and crossed the line.
We'll never hear them say why they lied:
No need for an inquiry—'no-one died'.

## Station 14: Laid in the Tomb

*Joseph took the body, wrapped it in a clean linen cloth, and placed it in his own new tomb that he had cut out of the rock. He rolled a big stone in front of the entrance to the tomb and went away.*

—Matthew 27:59-60

The squaddies played at pitch and toss,
*Hal an tow, Here we go!*
With Jesus nailed up on the cross,
They laughed below.

They gambled for his donkey jacket,
*Hal an tow, Here we go!*
The bastards fought for his fag packet,
They stooped that low.

And when he died there was a cry,
*Hal an tow, Here we go!*
The sun did hide her tearful eye,
So filled with woe.

The earth did tremble, pitheads fell,
*Hal an tow, Here we go!*
The soldiers nearly shat themselves:
See them go!

The pit wheels stopped, time stood still,
*Hal an tow, Here we go!*
On Calvary our Christ was killed
By wicked foes.

Lightning struck and cages rattled,
*Hal an tow, Here we go!*
With a great dragon he did battle.
How did that go?

So painful though his cuts may be,
*Hal an tow, Here we go!*
This mystery play's a comedy:
Ho, ho, ho!

They thought he'd taken his last breath,
*Hal an tow, Here we go!*
Miner Jesus mastered Death,
Gave blow for blow.

He went to hell and faced its gaffer,
*Hal an tow, Here we go!*
His spirit never died thereafter,
And it will grow!

They laid his body in a tomb
*Hal an tow, Here we go!*
A stone on top with no head room,
And buried low.

He dug him free through dirt and grass
*Hal an tow, Here we go!*
Came back to kick the buggers' arses,
A miracle, lo!

The NUM put up the fight,
*Hal an tow, Here we go!*
The rats went hiding from the light
As history knows.

Let's lift a pint, with songs rejoice,
*Hal an tow, Here we go!*
We'll sing defiance with one voice
And union show.

We'll raise a dram to toast the man,
*Hal an tow, Here we go!*
Born in a stall in Bethlehem,
Those years ago.

# After Hours: Fear No More

Based on Shakespeare's *Cymbeline*

*Fear no more the heat o the sun*

—*Cymbeline*, Shakespeare

*All go to one place. All are from the dust, and to dust all return.*

—Ecclesiastes 3:20

Fear no more the drop in the cage,
The crawl to the face, the din and the thrum.
Homeward you head with hard-won wage
Now your shift below is done,
When golden lads come from their shift,
To coal dust, ash, they surely drift.

Fear no more the frown of the boss,
No bully gaffer harms you now,
There is no fine, there is no loss,
Only one power to which you bow,
For wisdom, law, decree our kind,
Turns into ash, fades in the wind.

Fear no more the sudden flash,
Nor the dreaded fall of stone,
Fear not the tomb door's closing crash,
In darkness to be left alone.
All miners young, how much they graft,
Burn bright and flame then turn to ash.

But may your memory be well-known
And children learn about your days,
Your graves be green where grass is sown,
Your solidarity be praised,
May all your struggles now be past,
All souls like coal must turn to ash.

# Notes on the author and illustrator

**William Hershaw** is a Scots language makar and songwriter. Born in 1957, he was brought up in the former mining community of Cowdenbeath. He is the editor of *Lallans*, the Scots Language Society journal. His publications include *The Sair Road*, a poetic account of the 1984 Miners' Strike in Fife, and *McSuibne Agley*, a Scots Language version of the Irish Sweeney tale. He is the founder of The Bowhill Players, a folk group formed to continue the legacy of Joe Corrie, miner, poet and playwright, and to celebrate the rich culture of Fife's coalmining heritage.

**Les McConnell** was brought up in Ayrshire and attended Edinburgh College of Art in the sixties. He was awarded a postgraduate scholarship and studied in the Netherlands. He taught art for many years in Kirkcaldy, and his work has been exhibited widely including at the Royal Scottish Academy and the Society of Scottish Artists. He is a prizewinning book illustrator and has collaborated with William Hershaw on a number of books including *The Sair Road* and *Earth Bound Companions*.